MOVEMENT START

Over 100 Movement Activities and Stories for Children

First published in 2016 by
JemBooks
Cork,
Ireland
www.drama-in-ecce.com

ISBN: 978-0-9568966-6-7

Typesetting by Gough Typesetting Service, Dublin

All rights reserved.

No part of this book may be reproduced or utilised in any form or by any electronic, digital or mechanical means, including information storage, photocopying, filming, recording, video recording and retrieval systems, without prior permission in writing from the publisher. The only exception is by a reviewer, who may quote short excerpts in a review. The moral rights of the author have been asserted.

Text Copyright © 2016, Julie Meighan

MOVEMENT START

Over 100 Movement Activities and Stories for Children

Julie Meighan

JemBooks

About the Author

Julie Meighan is a lecturer in Drama in Education at the Cork Institute of Technology. She has taught Drama to all age groups and levels. She is the author of the Amazon bestselling *Drama Start: Drama Activities, Plays and Monologues for Young Children (Ages 3 -8)* ISBN 978-0956896605, *Drama Start Two: Drama Activities and Plays for Children (Ages 9-12)* ISBN 978-0-9568966-1-2 and *Stage Start: 20 Plays for Children (Ages 3-12)* ISBN 978-0956896629.

Contents

Introduction..1

PART ONE: MOVEMENT ACTIVITIES

Warm-Up Games

Here Today..6
Pass the Hat 6
Roll the Ball 7
Crossing the Circle..7
The Queen Bee..8
Four Corners...8
Musical Groups 9
Burst Balloon 9
Cat and Mouse..9
I Believe I Can Fly..10
Imagine you are..11
Movement Sequences 12

Imagination Games

Colour Movement..14
Animal Moves 14
Object Freeze 15
Monkey See, Monkey Do...16
Paint a Masterpiece 16
Magic Bouncing Balls..17
Barnyard Walk 18
Butterflies..18
Action Replay...19
Squirrels..19
What Can You Do with a Piece of String? 20
Dancing with Dance Fans 20
Captain May I?...20

Cooperation/Teamwork Games

Call and Response 22
Change the Movement 22
Action Charades 23
Sticky Balls 23
Balloon Keepy Ups 24
Human Knot 24
Dodge Ball 25
Freeze Tag 25
Bean Bag Freeze 25
Bacon 26
The Elephant's Trunk 26
Balloon Race Divide 27
Tug of War 27

Concentration Games

Who Stole the Cookies from the Cookie Jar? 30
Concentration—Are You Ready? 30
Move, Move, Pass It On 31
1 to 10 31
String Shapes 32
1, 2, 3, Clap 33
Mexican Move 33
Mirror! Mirror! 34
Back Chat 34
Ghost Hunters 34
Alien Invasion 35
The Bear and the Honey Pot 35

Coordination Games

Doors and Windows 38
Object Relay 38
Centipede 39
Bean Bag Balance 39
Pick Up the Bean Bag 40
Balloon Tennis 40
Bear Crawl 40
The Night at the Museum 41

Roll the Dice 41
The Troll's Bridge.. 42
Cooperative Chase 42
Ladders 43

Spatial Awareness Games

Threes.. 46
Snake's Tail 46
Egyptian Mummies 46
Buzzy Bees 47
Levels 47
Head to Head Dancing 48
Moving Together 48
Colour Jump 49
Alphabet Jump 49
Talk to the Hand 49

Observation Games

Movement Whispers 52
Hot Potato 52
Air Writing 53
Simon Says 53
Pass the Smile Around 53
Spud.. 54
This Is My Mouth 54
Movement Skipping 55
Find your Friend 55
Transport... 56
Sly Fox 56
Compass Points 57

Action Poetry/Songs

Do Your Ears Hang Low? 60
Little Bunny Foo Foo 61
Head, Shoulders, Knees and Toes 62
Five Little Speckled Frogs 63
My Body Action Song 65

When I Say 65
If You're Happy and You Know It 66
Five Little Monkeys 67
There Was a Princess Long Ago 69

PART TWO: MOVEMENT STORIES

Movement Story One: The Tortoise and the Hare 72
Movement Story Two: The Three Little Pigs 74
Movement Story Three: The Magical Music Shop 77
Movement Story Four: Rhino Chase 79
Movement Story Five: The Seed That Didn't Want to Grow 82
Movement Story Six: Adventure in Space 84
Movement Story Seven: The Clumsy Elephant and the Beautiful
  Ballet Shoes 87

Introduction:

Movement Start is a collection of movement activities, including games, action poems and stories, suitable for children between the ages of 3 and 8. It can be used in early years' settings or in primary schools. This book is also suitable for people working with children in any venue where movement is used, such as community groups, dance groups, drama classes, gymnastic clubs and so on.

The book is accessible and easy to follow. It is divided into two parts: Movement Activities and Movement Stories. Each section provides educators/facilitators/leaders with a variety of creative and imaginative ideas for stimulating movement activities in many different settings.

Part One: Movement Activities

There are eight different categories in this section. Each category, such as warm up games, states the main benefit of the activity it features. However, all of the activities in this book have more than one benefit. The games are clearly set out and the appropriate age group and minimum amount of children needed to participate are listed for each one. The other benefits of playing the game are also stated, and detailed instructions are provided, along with suggested extension for some of the games.

Warm-up Games

The main focus of these warm-up games is to prepare the children for kinaesthetic movement. In addition, warm ups help children to concentrate on the upcoming main activity. These games promote children's social interaction and teamwork skills. The games may be used as standalone activities; however, in order to achieve the optimum benefit they should be included as part of drama, movement or dance class. Ideally, they should be used to introduce or build a skill that is explored in the main class.

Game: Here Today
Age: 3 years+
Minimum number of participants: 4
Resources needed: Clear space.
Other benefits: Listening, concentration.
Instructions: The children form a circle by holding hands and they sit on the floor. The teacher says stand up and she stands up. All the children repeat the action and they stand up. The teacher says turn around and she turns around. The children repeat the action and they turn around. The teacher says sit down and she sits down. The children repeat the action and they sit down. When the teacher is confident that everyone knows the different actions she says "Child A is here today." When Child A hears his name he stands up, turns around and sits down. The teacher moves on to the next child and then she says "Child B" is here today." When "Child B" hears her name she stands up, turns around and sits down. This continues on until everyone in the circle has had an opportunity to stand up, turn around and sit down.

Game: Pass the Hat
Age: 3 years+
Minimum number of participants: 3
Resources needed: Clear space, a hat.
Other benefits: Listening, observation.
Instructions: The children sit in a circle and the teacher gives one of the children a hat. Everyone chants "Child A has the hat. What do you think of that? Take it off and pass it to Child B." Child A takes the hat off slowly and passes to Child B. The children continue with the chant until everyone has had a turn. The last child takes off the hat and puts it away safely.

Warm-up Games

Game: Roll the Ball
Age: 4 years +
Minimum number of participants: 3
Resources needed: Clear space, six balls of varying sizes.
Other benefits: Coordination, observation.
Instructions: Have the children sit in a tight circle on the floor with their legs spread out and their feet touching. The teacher rolls a ball to one of the children in the circle. The teacher calls out the child's name when she rolls the ball. The child who receives the ball rolls it to someone else. They call out the name of the child to whom they are rolling the ball. When the children are comfortable and seem at ease with the game, the teacher can gradually roll out more balls. The object of the activity is for the children to keep as many balls as possible rolling while still maintaining control.

Game: Crossing the Circle
Age: 4 years+
Minimum number of participants: 6
Resources needed: Clear space.
Other benefits: Observation, listening.
Instructions: Get the children to stand in a circle. The teacher gives each child a number—1, 2 or 3. The teacher calls out a number, for example "3". Everyone in the circle who has the number 3 must cross the circle and swap places with someone else who has the same number. Once they are familiar with crossing the circle, the teacher calls out a number as well as a way of moving.

Suggestions for ways of moving:
Stroll
Wander
March
Limp
Stagger
Crawl
Tiptoe
Stumble
Skip

If the children do not understand the word the teacher can explain what it means and demonstrate the movement. This can be a very good game for expanding vocabulary.

Game: The Queen Bee
Age: 3 years+
Minimum number of participants: 6
Resources needed: Clear space, pictures of different colour flowers.
Other benefits: Spatial awareness, colour recognition, listening, observation.
Instructions: The teacher spreads the flowers around the space. The children become bees. They move around the room buzzing like a bee and flapping their arms moving from one flower to the next gathering nectar. The teacher who is the queen bee calls out a colour such as red, and the bees must run as fast they can to collect all the red flowers and give them to the queen bee. The game continues until all the flowers are collected.

Game: Four Corners
Age: 4 years +
Minimum number of participants: 4
Resources needed: Clear space with four corners.
Other benefits: Listening, coordination.
Instructions: The teacher numbers each corner of the room from one to four. The teacher chooses a volunteer to be "it." "It" closes his/her eyes and counts aloud from ten to zero. Meanwhile, each child tiptoes silently to any one of the four corners of the room. Everyone must be in a corner by the time "It" says "zero," and then calls out a number of a corner before he/she opens their eyes. Children in that corner are out and return to their seats. The other children redistribute themselves and "It' counts again. Play continues until one child is left and he/she becomes the new "It." The teacher or the volunteer in the centre of the space can call out different ways of moving from the centre to the corner. The teacher can explain and demonstrate the movement if the children are unsure.

Suggestions for different ways of moving:
- Creep
- Dash
- Jog
- Dance
- Slide
- Glide
- Trudge
- Swim
- Fly

Game: Musical Groups
Age: 3 years+
Minimum number of participants: 4
Resources needed: Clear space, lively music.
Other benefits: Concentration, listening, number recognition, observation.
Instructions: All the children find their own space in the room. The children free dance to the lively music. When the music stops the teacher calls out a number such as "3." The children have to get into groups of three. They stay in their groups until the music starts again. They dance until the music stops and the teacher calls out another number. If there are any children left over and they are not in a group, they are out. Eventually all the children will be eliminated.

Game: Burst Balloon
Age: 4 years +
Minimum number of participants: 2
Resources needed: Clear space.
Other benefits: Relaxation, energy, concentration.
Instructions: The children lie on the floor. The teacher gets them to imagine that their body is a balloon. They are going to close their eyes and inflate the balloon. They fill up their tummies with air. Then, when they are full the teacher counts to three and the children shout "bang" and they let all the air out of their bodies like a deflated balloon.

Game: Cat and Mouse
Age: 3 years+
Minimum number of participants: 10
Resources needed: Clear space.
Other benefits: Observation, coordination.
Instructions: The whole group stands in a circle. One of the children volunteers to be the mouse. The mouse walks around the circle on the outside and taps someone on the shoulder. The child who is tapped on the shoulder becomes the cat. The cat tries to catch the mouse before she can get back to the cat's place in the circle.

Game: I Believe I Can Fly
Age: 4 years+
Minimum number of participants: 2
Resources needed: Clear space, pictures of objects and animals that can and can't fly (optional).
Other benefits: Body awareness, spatial awareness, concentration.
Instructions: Children sit in a circle and they discuss objects and animals that can fly. The teacher shows them pictures of things that can fly. Everyone stands up and the teacher calls the name of an object or an animal. If the object or animal can fly the children flap their arms and move around. If the object or thing cannot fly then the children stand on their tip toes and stretch their arms over their head.

Suggestions for objects/animals that can fly:
- Flies,
- Aeroplanes
- Bats
- Ladybirds
- Helicopters
- Bees
- Dragonflies
- Butterflies
- Eagles
- Moths
- Flying ants.

Suggestions for objects/animals that can't fly:
- Cars
- Emus
- Ducks
- Trains
- Caterpillars
- Worms
- Table
- Penguins
- Chickens
- House
- Tree
- Flowers.

Game: Imagine you are
Age: 3 years +
Minimum number of participants: 2
Resources needed: Clear space.
Other benefits: Imagination.
Instructions: This game helps children do traditional stretches in a creative and fun way. These stretches can be done individually or in pairs.

Imagine you are a whisk
Get the children to stand in a circle and put their hands over their head. They join their hands together and move them around in a large circle. Initially, they move their hands in a clockwise direction and when the group is comfortable moving in this direction, get them to move their hands in an anticlockwise direction.

Imagine you are an inchworm
Get the children to bend down and put their hands on the ground. Next, get them to walk their hands out in front of them until they are supporting their own body weight. The children get into a push-up position. They walk their feet up to their hands and then they continue walking their hands out and walking their feet up to their hands until they have moved to the other side of the room. Make sure that they have their own space and don't bump into one another.

Imagine you are a car wiper
Get the children to lie on the ground. When they are comfortable, get them to put their legs in the air. Slowly they move both legs from one side to another.

Imagine you are a cat stretching
Get the children to put their hands and feet on the floor, arch their back high in the air and stretch.

Imagine you are a giant
Get the children to take a big step and lunge on each step.

Imagine you are a marching soldier
Get the children to swing their arms and bring their knees up to their chest on each step.

Imagine you are a leaping frog
Get the children to squat down. They put their hands between their knees and jump around the space.

Extension: Get the children to use their creativity by getting them to imagine they are an object or animal. They have to devise a movement that represents their imagined object/animal.

Game: Movement Sequences
Age: 3 years+
Minimum number of participants: 2
Resources needed: Clear space.
Other benefits: Coordination, listening.
Instructions: The teacher discusses with the children different ways of moving. He/she asks the children to come up with as many ways to move as possible.

Suggestions for different ways to move:
- Walk
- Run
- Crawl
- Roll
- Hop
- Skip
- Jump
- Leap
- Tiptoe
- Tumble
- Turn
- Gallop
- Twirl
- Spin
- Walk sideways
- Walk backwards

The children will come up with many more ways of moving than those listed above. The teacher calls out different movement sequences such as:
- Walk-jump-twirl-tumble-run
- Spin-gallop-jump-skip-gallop

Extension: If the children are older then give them an opportunity to be the leader and call out their own movement sequences.

Imagination Games

Games that stimulate children's imagination provide them with an opportunity to role-play different situations. The following games not only stimulate creativity but they enhance social skills and empathy, as they allow the children to imagine themselves in someone else's shoes. Imagination is an important building block for increasing self-esteem and confidence. It helps children to use their own initiative and gives them control over the world they have created.

Game: Colour Movement
Age: 3 years +
Minimum number of participants: 4
Resources needed: Clear space, colour paper.
Other benefits: Colour recognition, observation, concentration.
Instructions: The teacher selects a variety of different colour paper and she/he assigns a movement concept to each colour. For example, red might imply "freeze/stop", blue could suggest "blowing" such as blowing in the wind, and green could signify "growth" like growing like a tree. When the teacher holds up different colour paper, the children should begin to perform the movement associated with it.

Extension: If the children are older, the teacher can ask them what movement concept they associate with different colours. They could come up with a variety of ways of moving for each colour.

Game: Animal Moves
Age: 3 years+
Minimum number of participants: 2
Resources needed: Clear space, pictures of various animals (optional).
Other benefits: Creativity, coordination, role-playing.
Instructions: The teacher gets the children to sit in a circle and introduces a variety of animals to them. The teacher may use some pictures of animals to engage the children and start the conversation. Get them to think about how the different animals move. Ask them what noise the different animals make. How do the animals interact with other animals? How they interact with children? As the teacher talks about the various animals, it may be a good idea to imitate their movements and the sounds they make. For example, a gorilla might pound his chest and make grunting noises. A bear might lumber around on all fours, growling. A bird might flap its wings and make cheeping or cawing noises. The children all sit in a circle and the teacher shows them a variety of animal pictures, such as a bear, gorilla, eagle, lion, elephant, etc. They discuss the various animals and how they move. Do they fly, jump, plod, crawl, and run? Do they move quickly or slowly? Do they move gracefully or awkwardly? The teacher gets the children y

To explore how the different animals move. The teacher could extend this game further by asking the children to make a sound with their movement. The children choose the animal they like and move around the space like the animal. They should interact with each other and react the way they believe their animal would. For example how would an elephant react if he saw a mouse? How would a deer react if he met a lion? How would a hippo react if he met a rhino?

Game: Object Freeze
Age: 3 years+
Minimum number of participants: 4
Resources needed: Clear space, lively music.
Other benefits: Listening, concentration.
Instructions: The children free dance to some lively music. When the music stops the teacher calls out an object and the children have to "freeze" in the shape of that object. If they move, they are out. The eliminated children get a chance to call out the object. You can use a theme. The following are some examples of different themes that could be used.

Halloween Freeze:
- Witch on her flying broomstick
- Bat flying in the night
- Zombie
- Frightened child
- Ghost
- Frankenstein
- Dracula
- Bobbling apple
- Pumpkin
- Cat

Superhero Freeze:
- Superman/Super Girl
- Batman/Batgirl
- Wonder Woman
- Iron Man
- Aqua man
- Wolverine
- The Hulk
- Flash
- Silver Surfer
- Thor

Circus Freeze:
- Ring Master
- Clown
- Juggler
- Knife Thrower
- Elephants
- Lion Tamer
- Lions
- Bears
- Magician
- Strongman

Game: Monkey See, Monkey Do
Age: 5 years+
Minimum number of participants: 2
Resources needed: Clear Space.
Other benefits: Coordination, observation.
Instructions: All the children sit in a circle. One of the children volunteers to be the monkey and enters the centre of the circle. The children chant the following rhyme:

> "Monkey, Monkey, we see you.
> Monkey, Monkey what can you do?"

The child in the centre of the circle makes a large movement and all the other children copy him while they chant…

> "Monkey, Monkey we see what you do.
> Monkey, Monkey we can do it too."

The child in the middle picks a new monkey. The game continues until everyone has had a turn.

Game: Paint a Masterpiece
Age: 6 years +
Minimum number of participants: 2
Resources needed: Clear space, music with different tempos.
Other benefits: Listening, vocabulary building.
Instructions: Get the children to find their own space. The teacher plays some music. The music can be a variety of different tempos. As the children listen to the music, they begin to imaginary paint what they hear. The teacher can tell them they don't have to paint people, places or objects; they can just paint colours or shapes if they want. Be sure to point out that whatever the children hear is what they should paint. Get them to listen very carefully.

Extension: For older children get them to listen for the changes in the music or listen for characters or events. When the music stops, the children stop painting. They hang up their imaginary painting on the wall and they describe their picture to the rest of the class.

Game: Magic Bouncing Balls
Age: 4 years+
Minimum number of participants: 4
Resources needed: Clear space, wand (optional).
Other benefits: Warm up, listening.
Instructions: Get each child to find a space. They must make sure they are not in each other's space. The teacher explains that the children are magic bouncing balls and she is a wizard with special powers. They all have to bounce up and down in their own space. When she waves her magic wand she can change them into anything she wants. If she says magic bouncing balls turn into roaring lions, they must all to turn into roaring lions. If she says magic bouncing balls turn into magic bouncing balls, the children turn themselves back into magic bouncing balls. The magic wizard can change the balls into anything she wants.

Suggestions:
- Television
- Chair
- Fairy
- Dinosaur
- Washing machine
- Tree
- Car
- Ballet dancer
- Hippo
- Monkey
- Lamp
- Phone
- Shark

Game: Barnyard Walk
Age: 3 years+
Minimum number of participants: 4
Resources needed: Clear space.
Other benefits: Warm ups, teamwork, role-playing.
Instructions: Encourage children to imitate different animals that are found on a farm. They move around the room like the animal they chose.
- Horse—gallop and neigh.
- Pig—roll on the floor (in the mud) and oink.
- Duck— waddle and quack.
- Rooster— pretend to fly and crow.
- Cow—moo and walk slowly.

Extension: In groups of three, get them to think of a farmyard animal and use their three bodies to make their chosen animal. One child could be the head, another could be the body, and another could be the legs. They have to move around the room, but they have to stay connected to one another while making the sound of the animal.

Game: Butterflies
Age: 3 years+
Minimum number of participants: 2
Resources needed: Classical music pieces, scarves.
Other benefits: Coordination, energy, focus, trust.
Instructions: Give each child two colourful scarves and encourage them to fly around like butterflies to the classical music. Butterflies is an excellent activity for children to use their imagination. Most children will love classical music if they are introduced to it at an early stage.

Suggestions of classical music pieces:
- *Carmen Overture,* Georges Bizet
- *In the Hall of the Mountain King,* Edward Grieg
- *The Flight of the Bumble Bee,* Nikolai Rimsky-Korsakov
- *The Teddy Bear's Picnic,* Henry Hall Orchestra
- *The Nutcracker,* Piotr Ilyich Tchaikovsky
- *Four Seasons,* Antonio Vivaldi
- *Carnival of the Animals,* Camille Saint Saens
- *Hoe-Down,* Aaron Copland
- *Hungarian Dance No.5,* Johannes Brahms

Game: Action Replay
Age: 4 years+
Minimum number of participants: 2
Resources needed: Clear space.
Other benefits: Imagination, communication.
Instructions: All the children begin by sitting in a circle. The group discusses different types of sports that they like to watch and/or play. Everyone chooses a sport and then they get up and find a space. They must act out a movement sequence based on their chosen sport. Everyone performs the movement sequence and then the teacher presses the button on her remote control and they have to do the same sequence in slow motion, fast forward and rewind.

Game: Squirrels
Age: 3 years+
Minimum number of participants: 6.
Resources needed: Clear space, hula hoops (one for each child), music.
Other benefits: Teamwork, observation focus.
Instructions: Get the children to imagine that they are squirrels. Tell them that in the autumn squirrels gather nuts and hide them so they will have enough food for the winter. Play some music and have children move to the music and pretend to be squirrels. They mime gathering nuts. Place the hula hoops around the room. The teacher informs the children that the hula hoops are the squirrel's home (dray). The squirrels must place their nuts in the hula hoops. When the music stops, the squirrels run to the hula hoops. Take away one hula hoop each time the music stops so that the squirrels have to share homes. Alternatively, you can sing the following song when they are collecting their nuts, and when the song ends they must run to the hula hoop. Eventually there will be only one hula hoop and they will all have to stand in it.

> **I'm a Little Squirrel** *(tune to I'm a little teapot.)*
> I'm a little squirrel, fuzzy and grey.
> When autumn comes, I gather nuts all day.
> So that when the winter comes, you see,
> I'll have food for my family and me.

Game: What Can You Do with a Piece of String?
Age: 5 years+
Minimum number of participants: 4
Resources needed: Clear space and a piece of sting for each team.
Other benefits: Teamwork, concentration, problem solving.
Instructions: Divide the class into groups of four. Give each group a piece of string. Give them three minutes to come up with as many things they can turn the piece of string into. For example, it could be a tightrope, a swimming pool, a rope in a tug of war, etc. At the end of the three minutes the groups must show the rest of the class the items that they turned their string into and use them. Each group gets a point for each original use of the string. The winner is the group with the most points.

Game: Dancing with Dance Fans
Age: 3 years +
Minimum number of participants: 2
Resources needed: Clear space, music, dance fans–you don't have dance fans, get some light, flowing material, scarves or ribbons and cut it into strips.
Other benefits: Listening, coordination.
Instructions: Give each child a dance fan and tell them to find their own space. If dance fans are not available then scarves or fabrics can be used instead. Alternatively, pieces of ribbon can be put on the end of a clothes peg and they will have the same effect. Play a variety of music and let the children move their dancing fans and bodies in response to it. For music suggestions see Butterflies in this section.

Game: Captain May I?
Age: 4 years+
Minimum number of participants: 4
Resources needed: Clear space.
Other benefits: Warm up, listening.
Instructions: This is a fun and popular game. One child volunteers to be the captain. The captain stands on the opposite side of room to the other children in the group who are all standing in a straight line. The captain then calls out a child's name and tells them what direction, step type and number of steps they must take. For example: "Anna, take two giants steps backwards." The chosen child has to ask "Captain, may I?" If the child doesn't ask the question then he/she is out of the game. The first one to reach and touch the captain wins and becomes the new captain. The captain must try to come up with imaginative ways of moving.

Cooperation/Teamwork Games

Cooperative activities help to develop children's ability to work successfully in a group. This process enables the children to improve patience, socialisation and their capacity to problem-solve. In order for these activities to be successful the children have to actively listen to one another and articulate their thoughts and ideas in a clear manner. The following activities help children to be a valuable part of a team which helps to promote confidence and self-esteem, as it gives them the opportunity to demonstrate their skills and abilities.

Game: Call and Response
Age: 4 years +
Minimum number of participants: 2
Resources needed: Clear space.
Other benefits: Creativity, focus, listening.
Instructions: Everyone sits in a circle. The teacher starts the activity by making a simple clapping rhythm. The rest of the circle repeats the rhythm. The child who is sitting next to the teacher takes a turn at making a simple clapping rhythm and the rest of the group copies it. When the group is comfortable with the call and response technique, the game can become a little more complicated. Each child must add to the clapping rhythm that has gone before them. The child who is last in the round must remember the clapping rhythm of everyone else before they do their own.

Extension: Older children can stand in a circle and use different parts of their bodies to make the rhythms. For example, they could use body percussion, stomping or tap dancing.

Game: Change the Movement
Age: 4 years +
Minimum number of participants: 6
Resources needed: Clear space.
Other benefits: Observation, concentration.
Instructions: All the children stand/sit in the circle. One of the children volunteers to go in the centre of the circle and be the detective. The detective closes his/her eyes and the teacher chooses a child to be the leader. The leader starts making a repetitive movement, like clapping hands or hopping on one leg. The detective opens his/her eyes and they must guess who the leader is. The leader can change the movement when the detective is not looking. The detective has three chances to guess who the leader is before the leader reveals themselves to the detective.

Game: Action Charades
Age: 4 years+
Minimum number of participants: 4
Resources needed: Clear space and a list of verbs.
Other benefits: Critical thinking, creativity.
Instructions: If there is a large number of children divide them into groups of 4 or 5. Give each group a verb, such as clean, cook or swim. One child will mime the verb to their group. The group members have a minute or two to guess the verb. To reduce noise, have one group participate at a time, while the other group members watch.

Suggestions of Verbs:
- Taste
- Smell
- Dance
- Jog
- Skate
- Scream
- Fight
- Cry
- Read
- Write
- Cook
- Clean
- Paint
- Joke
- Sleep
- Sneeze

Game: Sticky Balls
Age: 3 years+
Minimum number of participants: 6
Resources needed: Clear space.
Other benefits: Warm-up, observation.
Instructions: Have the children all bounce around in a defined area. When two children meet, they stick together and bounce together. Continue until all the children are stuck in one large ball.

Game: Balloon Keepy Ups
Age: 4 years +
Minimum number of participants: 2
Resources needed: Clear space, balloons.
Other benefits: Coordination, imagination, spatial awareness.
Instructions: Divide the group into smaller groups of six to eight, hand each group a balloon, and ask them to form a circle holding hands. The teacher tells them that, on her/his cue they are to put the balloon in the air between them and to keep it up using the body part the teacher calls (e.g., knees) without letting go of hands. They are to continue until the teacher calls out a different body part.

Suggestion of different body parts that can be used:
- Arms
- Legs
- Chest
- Elbows
- Fingers
- Knees
- Fists
- Nose
- Head
- Thighs
- Shoulders
- Face

Game: Human Knot
Age: 6 years+
Minimum number of participants: 8
Resources needed: Clear space.
Other benefits: Teamwork, coordination, warm-up.
Instructions: Children form a close circle. Each child grabs different hands across the circle, forming a tangle of arms. It is best if children grab different hands. Then, they must untangle the knot without letting go of each other's hands by moving arms over heads or stepping over arms. Sometimes, the untangled knot will form two circles, and sometimes it will be impossible to untangle. But most of the time they should be able untangle the knot.

Cooperation/Teamwork Games

Game: Dodge Ball
Age: 4 years+
Minimum number of participants: 4
Resources needed: Clear space, large soft ball.
Other benefits: Warm-up, focus, coordination.
Instructions: One child in the group is chosen to be the thrower. The child who is thrower has to throw the ball and hit the other children below the knee in order to catch them. The thrower can't run with the ball but once the thrower has succeeded in hitting one of the others, they both become throwers and can pass the ball between them, making the game more difficult for the other children. While the children can dodge the ball by jumping and running they cannot throw it. Only the children that have been caught can throw the ball.

Game: Freeze Tag
Age: 4 years+
Minimum number of participants: 4
Resources needed: Clear space.
Other benefits: Observation, coordination.
Instructions: One child volunteers to be the freezer. The freezer tries to catch the other children. Everyone else is running around. When the freezer catches someone, the child freezes in whatever position he/she got caught in. The child can be unfrozen by another child touching them on the shoulder. If a child gets caught three times then they become the freezer.

Game: Bean Bag Freeze
Age: 4 years+
Minimum number of participants: 4
Resources needed: Clear space, beanbags.
Other benefits: Co-operation, coordination.
Instructions: The children walk around the room slowly with a beanbag on their head. They try to avoid any objects or other children in the space. If the beanbag falls off the child's head, they have to freeze like a statue. Another child can pick the beanbag off the floor and put it back on the frozen child's head and he or she becomes unfrozen. This may be too difficult for younger children. If this is the case, then they just have to touch their shoulders to unfreeze the frozen children.

Game: Bacon
Age: 4 years+
Minimum number of participants: 8
Resources needed: Clear space and some object that represents the bacon.
Other benefits: Listening, observation.
Instructions: Divide the children into equal teams. The members of each team are numbered. They form two opposing lines and place the bacon in the exact centre between them. The teacher/facilitator then calls out a number. The children on each side who are assigned that number are the children for that round. No other team members leave their side of the field. Neither child may touch the other until someone touches the bacon. Once a child touches the bacon, however, the other child may catch him/her. If a child is able to grab the bacon and carry it back over to his/her own side, that team scores a point. If a child is caught after touching the bacon and before he/she returns to their own side, the team that caught the child scores a point. Note that the sequence of play usually involves two children running out and hovering over the bacon, waiting for a slight advantage to grab it and run back before the other child can react. The game is over when a predetermined number of points are scored, or when all numbers have been called.

Extension: The teacher can call more than one number, in which case several children from each side participate. In some games children may tag a child on the opposing team; in others, a child may only tag the child on the other team that they share a number with.

Game: The Elephant's Trunk
Age: 4 years+
Minimum number of participants: 4
Resources needed: Clear space.
Other benefits: Warm-up, coordination.
Instructions: Divide the group into pairs. Tell them that each pair is going to make an elephant's trunk. They do this by holding hands between their legs. They try to walk and they move from side to side. They must stay connected in the line. If they feel comfortable, get them to race each other. If they don't stay connected then they have to go back to the beginning.

Cooperation/Teamwork Games

Game: Balloon Race Divide
Age: 4 years+
Minimum number of participants: 8
Resources needed: A balloon for each group and a clear space.
Other benefits: Coordination, teamwork.
Instructions: Divide the group into teams. There should be at least four children in each team. Each child stands behind another. The child at the start of each line is given a balloon. The teacher calls out a part of the body and the children have to pass the balloon down the line just using that body part.

List of body parts suggestions:
- Head
- Arms
- Shoulders
- Hands
- Fingers
- Foot

Extension: Other dimensions could be included, such as passing the balloon standing on one leg, or sitting down without making eye contact.

Game: Tug of War
Age: 4 years+
Minimum number of participants: 6
Resources needed: Clear space.
Other benefits: Listening, imagination.
Instructions: Divide the class into two groups. Tell them they are going to imagine that they are holding a rope and they are going to mime a tug of war match. The rope is imaginary; however, it must not shrink or stretch. It must remain the same length throughout the match. The teacher can provide the commentary for the match and the children have to listen carefully and respond accordingly. The teacher decides who wins. When they are comfortable with the game then one of the group members can commentate on the match.

Concentration Games

It is important for the following concentration activities to be effective that a distraction free zone is created. Concentration skills help children's brain function, make complex tasks less frustrating and increase productivity due to the fact that freeing the mind and concentrating on the moment boosts cognition and helps one to focus completely on a task.

Game: Who Stole the Cookies from the Cookie Jar?
Age: 6 years+
Minimum number of participants: 4
Resources needed: Clear space.
Other benefits: Listening, name recognition.
Instructions: The group all sit in a circle. The group starts to alternate between clapping their hands and slapping their thighs.

The chant begins.

Group: Who *(claps hands)* stole *(slap thighs)* the cookie *(claps hands)* from the *(slaps thighs)* cookie *(claps hands)* jar *(slaps thighs)*.

Teacher: Annie *(claps hands)* stole *(slap thighs)* the cookie *(claps hands)* from the *(slaps thighs)* cookie *(claps hands)* jar *(slaps thighs)*.

Annie: Who, *(claps hands)* me? (Slaps thighs) Couldn't *(claps hands)* be *(slaps thighs)*.

Group: Then *(claps hands)* who? *(Slaps thighs)*.

Annie: Billy *(claps hands)* stole *(slap thighs)* the cookie *(claps hands)* from the *(slaps thighs)* cookie *(claps hands)* jar *(slaps thighs)*.

This continues on until everyone in the group has been accused of stealing the cookie from the cookie jar.

Game: Concentration—Are You Ready?
Age: 4 years +
Minimum number of participants: 4
Resources needed: Clear space.
Other benefits: Listening, memory.
Instructions: The children sit in a circle. The children clap their hands twice and click their fingers twice. Everyone numbers themselves. If there are 20 children in the group they would number themselves from one to 20. They start the chant.

Concentration *(clap twice)*, are you ready? *(Click your fingers twice)*. If so, *(clap hands twice)* let's go *(click fingers twice)*.

Number 1: 1 to 5. *(Keep the rhythm of the claps and clicking the fingers.)*
Number 5: 5 to 13.
Number 13: 13 to 20.

The children start to go faster and faster, and if a child makes a mistake or hesitates they are out. The more children that are out the less numbers to choose from, so they have to remember which numbers have been eliminated.

Concentration Games

Game: Move, Move, Pass It On
Age: 3 years+
Minimum number of participants: 4
Resources needed: Clear space.
Other benefits: Imagination, coordination.
Instructions: Everyone sits in a circle. The teacher teaches the group a song.

> *"Move, move, pass it on.*
> *Move, move, and pass it on.*
> *Move, move pass it on.*
> *Pass it around the circle."*

The words of the song are sung to the tune of "*Skip to the Lou.*"

Once the children are comfortable with the song, the teacher makes a simple movement, such as putting her hands on her head or folding her arms. She passes on the movement to the child on her left. The child passes on the movement to the child next to them until the move is passed around the circle. Everyone sings the song while the movement is being passed around. Everyone should get a chance to pass on a movement but just make sure every movement is different.

Extension: You could also replace the word "move" with "squeeze" or "clap" to simplify the game.

Game: 1 to 10
Age: 5 years +
Minimum number of participants: 8
Resources needed: Clear space.
Other benefits: Teamwork, observation.
Instructions: The children sit in a circle. They count from 1 to 10 together. Then they count from 10 to 1. Then they try to count from 1 to 10, jumping up when they say the number. Anyone can say the number, but if two children say a number and jump at the same time then the group must start from the beginning. When they have mastered 1 to 10, then they try to count in reverse from 10 to 1. To make this more difficult they can try to say the alphabet.

Game: String Shapes
Age: 4 years +
Minimum number of participants: 4
Resources needed: Clear space, a long piece of string for each group of four, blindfolds (optional).
Other benefits: Imagination, group cohesion, shape recognition.
Instructions: Divide the group into groups of 4. Give each group a long piece of string. Each member of the group is blindfolded (optional) or they close their eyes tightly. The teacher calls out a shape, such as square. Each group has to try to work together to make that shape with the string. The teacher gives them 30 seconds to complete. When the 30 seconds are up then the group stops and opens their eyes. The teacher decides which group has made the best shape square with their string and awards them a point. The group at the end of the game with the most points is the winner.

Shape suggestions:

Basic shapes
Circle
Square
Rectangle
Triangle
Oval

Advanced shapes
Trapezoid
Parallelogram
Pentagon
Hexagon
Octagon
Diamond
Star
Heart
Arrow
Crescent
Cube

Game: 1, 2, 3, Clap
Age: 3 years +
Minimum number of participants: 4
Resources needed: Clear space.
Other benefits: Coordination, listening.
Instructions: Everyone stands in the circle. Each child counts 1, 2, 3, clap 5, 6, 7, clap. Every fourth number the child must clap and not say the number. So number 4, 8, 12, 16, and 20 all must clap. Then in the second round the children say 1, 2, bend, clap, 5, 6, bend, clap. So number 3, 6, 9, 12, and 15 all must bend. On the third round they go 1, jump, bend, clap, 5, jump, bend, clap. The fourth round they say hop, jump, bend, and clap.

Game: Mexican Move
Age: 4
Minimum number of participants: 10
Resources needed: Clear space.
Other benefits: Focus, reflection.
Instructions: Children all start in a circle. They send a clap around the circle. Each child has to clap one after the other really quickly. The object is to get the clap around the circle as fast as possible. The teacher can time it. They can change the clap to a hop or a bend, or any other types of movement. They time each round and see which movement they get around the fastest.

List of movements:
Bend
Jump
Hop
Tiptoe
Roll
Skip
Slash
Carve

Game: Mirror! Mirror!
Age: 3 years+
Minimum number of participants: 2
Resources needed: Clear space.
Other benefits: Spatial awareness, warm-up.
Instructions: The group divides into pairs. They decide which one of them is "A," and which one is "B." The two children face each other. "A" starts moving slowly while "B" tries to do the same movement with the opposite side of his body like a mirror image. Children should continue the activity at various speeds for a few minutes then switch to "B" leading the exercise. Remind children to pay attention to their whole body and the body of their partner.

Game: Back Chat
Age: 4 years +
Minimum number of participants: 6
Resources needed: Clear space.
Other benefits: Body awareness, recognition of shapes, numbers, letters.
Instructions: Divide the class into two groups. Both groups stand in a line with their back to the child behind them. The teacher gives the children at the end of each group a letter. They write that letter with their finger on the back of the child in front of them. The child at the end of the line has to say the letter. If the group gets the letter correct they get a point. Shapes, numbers, or words could be used if the group finds letters too easy.

Game: Ghost Hunters
Age: 3 years +
Minimum number of participants: 4
Resources needed: Clear Space.
Other benefits: Listening, observation.
Instructions: One of the children volunteers to be the ghost. The rest of the group find their own space in the room and they close their eyes. The ghost tries to turn as many children as possible in to ghosts by standing behind them for 10 seconds. If a child says "is there a ghost behind me" then they are safe. If the ghost successfully stands behind a child for 10 seconds without having been detected then that child turns into a ghost, moves around the room and tries to stand behind other children for 10 seconds without being detected. Eventually, everyone will be a ghost and they move around in ghostly and haunting manner.

Game: Alien Invasion
Age: 6 years +
Minimum number of participants: 6
Resources needed: Clear space, balloons or beanbags which represent the bombs.
Other benefits: Communication, listening, teamwork.
Instructions: Get the group to imagine that they are aliens. They want to drop some bombs on Mars. They have to drop the bombs without them exploding or else they will all die. They are three groups and they must communicate with each other successfully in order for the mission to be successful.

Group 1: They can't talk or move. They can communicate through body language.

Group 2: They can talk but not move.

Group 3: They can move and talk but they are blind. They can be blindfolded or close their eyes if they are more comfortable with this.

The objective is that group 1 communicates with group 2 by body language. Group 2 communicates with group 3 through speech, and group 3 must find the bombs and move them from one designated part of the room to another.

Game: The Bear and the Honey Pot
Age: 4 years+
Minimum number of participants: 4
Resources needed: Clear Space and blindfold (optional).
Other benefits: Listening, warm-up,
Instructions: Everyone sits in a circle. One child volunteers to be the bear. The bear sits in the centre of the circle. There is an object that represents a honey pot in front of the bear. All the other children are bees. The bear can't see. (The bear can be blindfolded or just have his/her eyes closed.) Although the bear can't hear, he/she has very good hearing. When the teacher points at a bee they must get up slowly and try to retrieve the honey pot without the bear hearing them. If the bear hears the bee he can point at them and they have to freeze in that position. If one of the bees is successful at retrieving the honey pot without the bear pointing at them then he/she is the bee for the next round.

Coordination Games

The activities in this section promote the following types of coordination skills:

Gross motor coordination: This type of coordination is the movement of arms, legs and body that allows children to walk, run, jump, throw, kick and twist.

Fine motor coordination: This type of coordination allows children to perform tasks that require precision. Activities that require children to manipulate small objects will improve their fine motor skills.

Hand-eye coordination: This type of coordination allows children to guide their hand to complete a task.

Many of the following activities integrate the three types of coordination.

Game: Doors and Windows
Age: 5 years+
Minimum number of participants: 10
Resources needed: Clear space.
Other benefits: Spatial awareness, group work.
Instructions: The children form a circle while standing and holding their hands. The group spreads out enough so that everyone's arms are straight in the circle. This should form large spaces between the circle members. These large spaces represent the windows and doors. Then one child is chosen to be the runner. The runner starts running, and weaving in and out between the windows and doors. The children in the circle randomly drop their arms down trying to touch or trap the runner who is weaving his/her way in and out of the windows and doors. Once the runner is caught or touched by the arms of someone in the circle, they are out. The runner chooses another child in the group to take his/her place and they become the next child to weave in and out of the windows and doors.

Game: Object Relay
Age: 5 years +
Minimum number of participants: 4
Resources needed: Clear space, a ball and a variety of objects (optional).
Other benefits: Imagination, teamwork, focus.
Instructions: Children stand in a line. If there are lots of children in the class you make more than one line. Each line has a ball. The ball must be passed down the line. The teacher calls out the instruction of how the ball should be passed down the line. Once the ball gets to the end of the line it has to be passed back.

Suggested instructions:
- *Pass the ball overhead.*
- *Pass the ball between your legs.*
- *Pass the ball without using your hands.*
- *Pass the ball by just using your chest.*
- *Pass the ball by just using your head.*

If a team drops the ball then they have to go back to the beginning.

Extension: You could have a box of different objects that they must pass down the line. Each line should have the same objects. The line that gets all the objects down safely is the winner.

Coordination Games

Game: Centipede
Age: 5 years +
Minimum number of participants: 5
Resources needed: Clear space.
Other benefits: Teamwork, trust.
Instructions: Divide the group into groups of 5 or 6. The children in each group sit on the floor and hold the ankles of the child behind them. They call out left, right and the group has to try to move while everyone is holding the ankles of the child in front of them. If there is more than one group they can have a centipede race.

Game: Bean Bag Balance
Age: 4 years +
Minimum number of participants: 2
Resources needed: Clear space, bean bags for each member of the class.
Other benefits: Focus, imagination, problem solving.
Instructions: The teacher gets the children put a bean bag on their heads and they walk slowly around the room. Once they feel comfortable the children can walk faster and faster. They can see if they can run with the bean bag on their head. Once they have mastered balancing the beanbags on their head then they can see if they can balance the bean bag on other parts of their body.

Suggested Body Parts:
- *Knees*
- *Foot*
- *Hands*
- *Thighs*
- *Shoulder*
- *Face*
- *Wrist*
- *Toes*

Again, they start off slowly and then they get faster and faster. The child that can balance on the most body parts and move the fastest is the winner.

Game: Pick Up the Bean Bag
Age: 3 years +
Minimum number of participants: 2
Resources needed: Clear space and a variety of bean bags, a basket or box for each child.
Other benefits: Warm up, teamwork.
Instructions: The teacher gets a variety of bean bags and spreads them across the space. The children have 10 seconds to see how many beanbags they can collect. The group could divide into sub-groups of three or four and have a race to see who can pick up the most beanbags in the time allotted.

Game: Balloon Tennis
Age: 3 years+
Minimum number of participants: 2
Resources needed: Clear space, balloons, empty kitchen rolls.
Other benefits: Observation, spatial awareness.
Instructions: Give each child a balloon and an empty kitchen roll. The teacher shows the children how to keep the balloon up with the kitchen roll. In pairs they can hit the balloon to one another.

Game: Bear Crawl
Age: 3 years+
Minimum number of participants: 2
Resources needed: Clear space.
Other benefits: Spatial awareness, body awareness.
Instructions: The teacher asks the children how a bear crawls, and then tells them to imagine that they are bears crawling through the forest. They get down on their hands and knees. The children are told that they can't put their knees on the ground. They start moving forwards. When they are comfortable with the movement the group can have bear-crawl races or bear-crawl relays. Mark a starting line, and a finish line 10 metres away.

Coordination Games

Game: The Night at the Museum
Age: 4 years +
Minimum number of participants: 4
Resources needed: Clear space.
Other benefits: Imagination, trust, role-play, observation.
Instructions: The teacher/facilitator or one of the children volunteers to be a security guard. All the children spread out and become a selected museum artefact. They make a sculpture of their chosen artefact. The security guard walks around the space. When his/her back is turned the children change position. If the children are seen they are removed from the display floor. The last child left becomes the new security guard.

Suggestion of different types of museums:
- *Waxworks*
- *Prehistoric*
- *Art*
- *Dinosaur*
- *Science*
- *Music hall of fame*

Game: Roll the Dice
Age: 3 years+
Minimum number of participants: 2
Resources needed: Clear space, a dice for each member of the group.
Other benefits: Creativity, memory, focus.
Instructions: Everyone rolls their dice together. Each number corresponds to action such as:

1 Wiggle your body for 10 seconds.
2 Spin around 5 times.
3 Stand on your right leg for 15 seconds.
4 Hop 10 times.
5 Make a large circle with your arms 10 times.
6 Close your eyes and take 5 deep breaths.

Once the children have become used to the actions, get them to come up with their own actions for each number.

Game: The Troll's Bridge
Age: 4 years +
Minimum number of participants: 3
Resources needed: Masking tape, objects to carry.
Other benefits: Energy, focus.
Instructions: Make a bridge with the masking tape. Tell the children that they are crossing a very narrow bridge and there is a troll that lives underneath it. The children are crossing the bridge going to visit their friend. They are carrying a variety of objects with them. The children are told the troll won't bother them if they stay on the narrow bridge and don't drop anything. If they fall off the bridge or drop anything then the troll chases them. The troll can be the teacher or another child. If you want to make it more difficult tell them to carry the objects over the bridge on their head.

Game: Cooperative Chase
Age: 3 years +
Minimum number of participants: 6
Resources needed: Clear space.
Other benefits: Warm-up, teamwork.
Instructions: One child volunteers to be "It." If he catches another child in the group then they join together and connect. The connected pair need to work together to catch a third child who in turn would connect to them. They do it until everyone is connected. If the group catches someone and the connection is broken, then that child is free to go.

Game: Ladders
Age: 5 years +
Minimum number of participants: 2
Resources needed: Clear space, 20 rulers or sticks.
Other benefits: Warm-up, teamwork.
Instructions: Divide the class into two teams. Each team has ten sticks (rulers optional). The teacher uses the sticks to create two ladders so that there is one ladder for each team. One child from each team hops over the sticks without touching any of them. If a stick is touched, the child has to go back to the beginning of the ladder and starts again. When the child has hopped over all the sticks he stops, still on one foot, and bends down to pick up the last stick. He then turns around and hops over the sticks back to the beginning. When he reaches the start point he drops the stick and the next child hops over the nine remaining sticks. Each team continues until all of the sticks have been picked up. The team that finishes with the fastest time is the winner.

Spatial Awareness Games

Developing spatial awareness is important in order for children to understand their space and the location of objects in relation to their body. When children develop spatial awareness they become aware of concepts such as direction, distance and place.

Game: Threes
Age: 4 years +
Minimum number of participants: 3
Resources needed: Clear space.
Other benefits: Teamwork, socialisation, imagination.
Instructions: Get the children into groups of three. Give them instructions to make themselves as tall as they can as a group and then as small as they can. Then have them make a vertical shape, horizontal shape or a diagonal shape as a group of three. Next have them make different utensils with their bodies, such as a spoon, fork or knife.

Game: Snake's Tail
Age: 4 years +
Minimum number of participants: 6
Resources needed: Clear space.
Other benefits: Group cohesion, creativity.
Instructions: The children all line up one behind the other in single file. They place their hands on the shoulders of the child in front of them. The teacher tells them to imagine that they are one large snake and the child in front is the head of the snake and the last child in the line is the tail of the snake. When the teacher shouts "go" the head tries to capture the tail. However, the line has to stay connected throughout the chase. When the head catches the tail, the tail becomes the head and it starts all over again. The group continues until each child has an opportunity to be both the head and the tail.

Game: Egyptian Mummies
Age: 5 years +
Minimum number of participants: 4.
Resources needed: Clear space, lots of toilet rolls.
Other benefits: Cooperation, body awareness.
Instructions: Divide the group into pairs. Give each pair a toilet roll. Child A becomes the mummy and Child B does the mummifying. Child B wraps the mummy with the toilet roll. When they are finished the teacher asks them how the mummy would move, and how and why its movement would be restricted? Then all the mummies must catch the other children. When they are done the other children become the mummies.

Spatial Awareness Games

Game: Buzzy Bees
Age: 3 years +
Minimum number of participants: 2
Resources needed: Clear space, construction paper to make the flowers and music.
Other benefits: Teamwork, imagination, role-playing.
Instructions: The teacher needs to make flowers with coloured construction paper before the activity takes place. The flowers are randomly spread around the room. The children imagine that they are bees. They must fly and buzz using fast movements. They fly from flower to flower collecting nectar. Play some music and when the music stops the children have to freeze on a flower. The flowers can be taken away one by one until eventually all the bees need to freeze on one flower. At least one part of their body needs to be on the flower, otherwise they are out. They must work together so they don't lose any of the bees.

Game: Levels
Age: 4 years+
Minimum number of participants: 2
Resources needed: Clear space.
Other benefits: Imagination, role-playing, observation, focus.
Instructions: Get the children to move around the room at different heights. Tell them to try to move in a normal fashion, then as tall as they can make themselves, and then as small as they make themselves. The teacher tells the children they can move around the room anyway they want but at the height of the noun that he\she calls outs. For example, if the teacher calls out a snake the children should be moving on the floor. If a giraffe is called they should move around as tall as they can.

Suggested nouns:
- *Television*
- *Chair*
- *Car*
- *Horse*
- *Elephant*
- *Snail*
- *Mouse*
- *Dog*
- *Table*
- *Fire*
- *Candle*

Game: Head to Head Dancing
Age: 4 years+
Minimum number of participants: 2
Resources needed: Clear space, music.
Other benefits: Listening, cooperation.
Instructions: Divide the group into pairs. The teacher puts on some music and the children dance in pairs and when the music stops they freeze. The teacher then tells them they must do head-to-head dancing. They must connect their heads together and dance together when the music comes on without losing their connection. The teacher shouts out different body parts and then the children have to connect those body parts together while they are dancing.

Suggested body parts:
- *Shoulder to shoulder*
- *Back to back*
- *Elbow to elbow*
- *Knee to knee*
- *Nose to nose*
- *Ear to ear*

Game: Moving Together
Age: 5 years +
Minimum number of participants: 3
Resources needed: Clear space.
Other benefits: Problem solving, teamwork.
Instructions: The children get into groups of three. They must move from one side of the space to the other side but they have to be connected. The teacher gives the following instructions:

How do you move?
- With only three feet touching the ground
- With only your heads connected
- With two noses on the ground
- With two heads, three legs and two hands and an elbow on the ground

The teacher can use his/her imagination or they can appoint one of the groups to give instructions to the other groups.

Spatial Awareness Games

Game: Colour Jump
Age: 3 years+
Minimum number of participants: 2
Resources needed: Clear space.
Other benefits: Listening, observation, focus.
Instructions: Ask the children to look at their clothing. Ask them to notice the colours they are wearing. Tell the children that when you name a colour they are wearing they will jump up and then sit back down. Be sure the children have enough space to move without hurting other children. If your space is limited, they can all stand and then hop when a colour their wearing is called.

Game: Alphabet Jump
Age: 4 years+
Minimum number of participants: 2
Resources needed: Clear space.
Other benefits: Listening, focus.
Instructions: Tell the children that you are going to name a letter of the alphabet. When a child's name begins with that letter, that child can jump up and then sit back down. Recite the alphabet, and pause when you reach a letter that begins a child's name. If that child hesitates, repeat the letter and look at the child. You can prompt a child by saying, "B. B. I think Bryan starts with B."

Game: Talk to the Hand
Age: 6 years+
Minimum number of participants: 2
Resources needed: Clear space.
Other benefits: Spatial awareness, observation, focus.
Instructions: Divide the group into pairs. One child is the leader and the other is the follower. The leader must place their hands about a quarter of a metre away from the follower's face. The leader must then lead the follower around the room slowly by moving their hand. They should aim to make sure they keep the same distance between the hand and the face throughout the game. The children should be aware of all the other pairs in the group as they move around the room and they must try not to bump into anyone. After a few minutes they can reverse the roles so that each one of them gets a chance to become a leader and a follower.

Observation Games

Observation refers to the act of watching or noticing. If children develop their observation skills they enhance their awareness of the world around them. Observation improves communication and socialisation skills because it increases empathy, and allows a child to see things from other people's perspectives. With good observation skills comes an increase in attention span. Group working skills improve as the children are able to see the larger picture.

Game: Movement Whispers
Age: 5 years +
Minimum number of participants: 4
Resources needed: Clear space.
Other benefits: Coordination, concentration.
Instructions: The children all line up in single file, one directly behind the other. All the children should be looking at the back of the child in front of them. The teacher makes a movement to Child A, who is last in the line. Child A then taps the shoulder of Child B in front of him who turns around. Then Child A copies the movement that the teacher made and Child B observes the movement and then turns around and taps the shoulder of Child C in front of him and makes the movement. The movement is passed down the line until the last child must make the movement and it should be the same as the original movement made by the teacher.

Suggested large movements:
- *Move from side to side three times*
- *Jump up and down in slow motion*
- *Bend your knees quickly 5 times*
- *Punch the air with your fist*
- *Shake your whole body out*
- *Put your hands over your head and stretch your whole body out*
- *Swing both arms around together twice*
- *Turn around three times and sit down.*

Game: Hot Potato
Age: 3 years +
Minimum number of participants: 2
Resources needed: A balloon/ball and a clear space.
Other benefits: Teamwork.
Instructions: The balloon or ball represents the potato. The potato is too hot and nobody wants to touch it. The teacher throws the potato up into the air. The potato must not hit the ground. The children can try to keep the potato off the ground when they are standing, standing in a circle, sitting, touching the ground with one knee, lying on their backs, hopping on one leg, or jumping up and down.

Game: Air Writing
Age: 5 years +
Minimum number of participants: 2
Resources needed: Clear space.
Other benefits: Creativity, focus.
Instructions: Divide the group into pairs. Each pair stands opposite each other. Child A writes a letter in the air and (the movements have to be large and exaggerated). Child B has to guess it within a 30-second time frame. If the children find the letters too easy then they can do numbers, words or they can draw pictures. The pair that has the most correct answers is the winner.

Game: Simon Says
Age: 3 years +
Minimum number of participants: 2
Resources needed: Clear space.
Other benefits: Listening, concentration.
Instructions: One child volunteers to be Simon and starts by saying, "Simon says, 'touch your nose.'" Everyone must then do the action. However, if Simon makes an action request without saying "Simon says" to begin the request, anyone who does that action is out. The child still playing at the end will be Simon for the next round.

Game: Pass the Smile Around
Age: 4 years +
Minimum number of participants: 3
Resources needed: Clear space.
Other benefits: Focus, communication.
Instructions: The game begins with everyone sitting in a circle. Child A smiles at everyone round the circle, trying to make someone else giggle or laugh. He gets a point for everyone who can't keep a totally straight face. After a while, he uses one hand to literally "wipe" the smile off his face, and hand it to the child next to him in the circle.

Extension: This activity can be made more difficult for older children. Instead of a smile they can pass different emotions around the circle, such as anger, excitement, surprise, delight, sadness, happiness, and so on. The objective is to be aware of the movement they use on their face and body in order to express different emotions.

Game: Spud
Age: 5 years+
Minimum number of participants: 6
Resources needed: A large space preferably in a sport's hall or outside.
Other benefits: Warm-up.
Instructions: This is a well-known children's game that has been played in the playground for many years. Each child is given a number and they closely surround the child who has been chosen to be on. The child who is on then tosses the ball straight up and the other children run away. As the ball reaches the top of its toss, the child that is on calls out the number of one of the other players and then runs away. The child whose number was called must run back and catch the ball. Once that child has the ball, they shout, "Spud!" Then everyone else must freeze. The child with the ball must try to hit one of the children with the ball. If they do it successfully, then the child who has been hit by the ball gets a letter: First S, then P, then U, and then D, and is on for the next round. If they miss, the child who threw the ball is on for the next round.

Game: This Is My Mouth
Age: 7 years+
Minimum number of participants: 4
Resources needed: Clear space.
Other benefits: Focus, imagination.
Instructions: The children sit in a circle. The teacher starts by pointing to her head and saying "this is my mouth." The child next to the teacher in the circle points at her mouth and says "this is my head," and then goes on to point to her elbow and says "this is my knee. The next child then points at her knee and says "this is my elbow" and goes on to say "this is my finger" and points to her toe. This goes on around the circle until everyone gets a chance. The children have to listen very carefully because the game can get confusing.

Game: Movement Skipping
Age: 4 years+
Minimum number of participants: 2
Resources needed: Clear space.
Other benefits: Concentration.
Instructions: The teacher performs a movement and all the children watch carefully. Then the teacher performs another movement. The children perform the first movement. The teacher performs the third movement and the children perform the second movement. If a child performs the wrong movement they are out. The last child standing becomes the leader for the next round. The movements can get faster as soon as the children have grasped the concept.

For example: Teacher's first movement is to bend her knees.
Teacher's second movement: Clap her hands.
Teacher's third movement: Stomp her feet.
Children's first movement: Bend their knees
Children's second movement: Clap their hands.
Children's third movement: Stomp their feet.

Game: Find your Friend
Age: 3 years+
Minimum number of participants: 8
Resources needed: Clear space.
Other benefits: Warm-up, creativity, role-playing.
Instructions: Everyone stands in a circle and closes their eyes. The teacher walks around the circle and taps the children on different parts of the body. If she taps a child on the head they become a bear. If she taps the child on the back they become a dinosaur. If she taps the children on the shoulder they become mice. If she taps the children on the elbow they become lions. Finally, if she taps the children on the hand they become dragons. When everyone has been assigned an animal the teacher counts to three and all the children open their eyes and they move around the room as their animal would. They must see if they can recognise the children who are the same animal as themselves, and form a group with them. After a few minutes the teacher will shout "freeze" and see if they are in the right group.

Game: Transport
Age: 3 years+
Minimum number of participants: 2
Resources needed: Clear space, pictures of different modes of transport.
Other benefits: Spatial awareness, imagination.
Instructions: The children sit in a circle and the teacher shows them pictures of different types of transport. They discuss how the different modes of transport move. Each child has to choose to be a different mode of transport. The teacher tells the children to find their own space and that they are going to move around like their chosen transportation method. Make sure they understand the rules of the road. They can't bump into anyone else; if they do, their licence will be taken off them and they will be banned from the game for 1 minute. Tell them to turn on their engine and rev it up. Then they move like their chosen form of transport. The teacher will call out different ways of moving.

Suggested ways of moving:
- *Reverse*
- *Go over speed bumps fast*
- *Go uphill slowly*
- *Go downhill*
- *Make a sharp turn*
- *Make an emergency stop*
- *Avoid an oncoming speeding car*
- *Go fast but slow down at speeding lights*
- *Come to a complete stop at a red light*

Game: Sly Fox
Age: 3 years+
Minimum number of participants: 4
Resources needed: Clear space.
Other benefits: Listening, spatial awareness.
Instructions: One child is chosen or volunteers to be the fox and stands with their back to the rest of the group, who are at the other end of the space. The children try to sneak up quietly behind the fox without being spotted. The fox turns around at random intervals to try to catch someone moving. If he sees a child moving he calls out their name and they have to go back to the start. To win, one of the children must succeed in touching the fox without having been seen. The winner becomes the sly fox in the next round.

Game: Compass Points
Age: 4 years+
Minimum number of participants: 3
Resources needed: Clear space.
Other benefits: Listening, coordination.
Instructions: Assign each wall in the space a point on the compass. North, south, east, or west. When the teacher calls one of these points the children have to run to them. Once they have got used to it then the teacher can make it more complicated by calling different combinations, such as south and east, north and west, south and west, north and east. The children have to run to both points. The child who reaches the point last is eliminated. If a child runs to the wrong point then they are out. The last child is the winner and they can call out the compass points for the next game.

Action Poetry/Songs

The following are some well-known and fun action poems/songs that can be introduced to children from an early age. Integrating action poetry/songs to a movement, dance or drama lesson has many benefits. In addition to developing children's coordination skills, action poetry/songs enhance auditory, listening and memorisation skills. The imaginative characters and the creative stories that are found in these poems enable children to expand their imagination and introduce them to the world of storytelling, and to the land of fantasy and make believe.

Do Your Ears Hang Low?

Directions: This is a popular and fun action poem/song. The children find their own space. The teacher tells the children that they are to imagine that they are a little rabbit. Get them to make bunny ears with their hands. Before the poem/song starts everyone must show their ears.

Do your ears hang low? *(Children use their hands to represent their ears. They move their hands downwards.)*

Do they wobble to and fro? *(Children move their ears forward and backward.)*

Can you tie them in a knot? *(Children tie an imaginary knot.)*

Can you tie them in a bow? *(Children tie an imaginary bow.)*

Can you throw them o'er your shoulder like a continental soldier? *(Children toss something over their shoulder and then they salute.)*

Do your ears hang low? *(Children move their hands downward.)*

Do your ears hang high? *(Children move their hands upward.)*

Do they reach up to the sky? *(Children reach their hands up, to the sky.)*

Do they droop when they are wet? *(Children relax their bodies.)*

Do they stiffen when they're dry? *(Children stiffen up their whole bodies.)*

Can you throw them o'er your shoulder like a continental soldier? *(Children toss something over their shoulder and then they salute.)*

Do your ears hang high? *(Children move their hands upward.)*

Do your ears hang out? *(Children move their hands out to the side.)*

Can you waggle them about? *(Children flap their hands.)*

Can you flip them up and down as you fly around the town? *(Children fly around their space.)*

Can you throw them o'er your shoulder like a continental soldier? *(Children toss something over their shoulder and then they salute.)*

Do your ears hang out? *(Children move their hands out to the side.)*

Action Poetry/Songs

Little Bunny Foo Foo

Directions: Little Bunny Foo Foo can be recited as a poem or can be sung along to the tune of the famous Canadian children's song *Alouette*. This poem can also be used as a role-playing game by the teacher picking a child to be Little Bunny Foo Foo, and another child to be Blue Fairy. The rest of the children could be the field mice.

Little Bunny Foo Foo *(Children make bunny ears with their hands.)*

Hopping through the forest. *(Children hop up and down.)*

Scooping up the field mice *(Children mime scooping up the mice with their fists.)*

And bopping them on the head. *(Children hit their hands.)*

Down came the good fairy and the Good Fairy said: "Little Bunny Foo Foo I don't want to see you

Scooping-up the field mice and bopping them on the head!" *(Children shake their heads and wag their fingers.)*

"I'm going to give you three chances then I'll turn you into a goon!" *(Children show the number of chances with their fingers.)*

The next day *(pause)*

Little Bunny Foo Foo *(Children make bunny ears with their hands.)*

Hopping through the forest. *(Children hop up and down.)*

Scooping up the field mice *(Children mime scooping up the mice with their fists.)*

And bopping them on the head. *(Children hit their hands.)*

Down came the Good Fairy, and the Good Fairy said: "Little Bunny Foo Foo, I don't want to see you scooping up the field mice and bopping them on the head!" *(Children shake their heads and wag their fingers.)*

"I'm going to give you three chances then I'll turn you into a goon!" *(Children show the number of chances with their fingers.)*

The next day *(pause)*

Little Bunny Foo Foo *(Children make bunny ears with their hands.)*

Hopping through the forest. *(Children hop up and down.)*

Scooping up the field mice *(Children mime scooping up the mice with their fists.)*

And bopping them on the head. *(Children hit their hands.)*

Down came the Good Fairy and the Good Fairy said: "Little Bunny Foo Foo I don't want to see you scooping up the field mice and bopping them on the head!" *(Children shake their heads and wag their fingers.)*

"I gave you three chances and I'm going to turn you into a goon!"

POOF! *(All the children turn into goons.)*

Head, Shoulders, Knees and Toes

Directions: Everyone stands in a circle. The teacher points to different parts of the body. The teacher says

Head. *(Everyone point to your head.)*
Shoulders. *(Everyone point to your shoulders.)*
Knees. *(Everyone point to your knees.)*
Toes. *(Everyone point to your toes.)*
(Repeat)
Eyes. *(Everyone point to your eyes.)*
Ears. *(Everyone point to your ears.)*
Mouth. *(Everyone point to your mouth.)*
Nose. *(Everyone point to your nose.)*

When everyone in the group has practiced the movements the song can begin. Sing or recite the words three times. The first time everyone says it slowly, the second time get them to go faster and the third time they must say it as fast as they can. The objective is for the group to keep together.
Head, shoulders, knees and toes, knees and toes
and eyes and ears and mouth and nose.
Head, shoulders, knees and toes, knees and toes. *(Recite/sing and do the actions at a slow pace.)*

Head, shoulders, knees, and toes, knees and toes
and eyes and ears and mouth and nose.
Head, shoulders, knees and toes, knees and toes. *(Recite/sing and do the actions at a normal pace.)*

Head, shoulders, knees, and toes, knees and toes
and eyes and ears and mouth and nose.
Head, shoulders, knees and toes, knees and toes. *(Recite/sing and do the actions at a fast pace.)*

Action Poetry/Songs

Five Little Speckled Frogs

Directions: The group sits in a circle. The circle represents a pool. Five children volunteer to be the five speckled frogs. The five frogs sit in the centre of the circle in a straight line as if they are sitting on a log. The frogs are numbered from one to five and they must listen carefully for their number. The rest of the children are going to recite the poem and frogs are going to do the actions.

Five little speckled frogs sat on a speckled log. (*The five frogs are sitting on the log.*)

Eating some most delicious bugs. (*The five frogs mime catching and eating bugs*).

Yum, yum! (*The five frogs rub their tummies.*)

One jumped into the pool. (*Frog 1 hops up and jumps into the pool.*)

Where it was nice and cool (*Frog 1 swims in the pool for the duration of the poem*).

Then there were four speckled frogs. (*Each of the four remaining frogs hops up and sits down on the log.*)

Glug, glug! (*The four frogs make a glugging sound.*)

Four little speckled frogs sat on a speckled log. (*The four frogs are sitting on the log.*)

Eating some most delicious bugs. (*The four frogs mime catching and eating bugs.*)

Yum, yum! (*The four frogs rub their tummies.*)

One jumped into the pool. (*Frog 2 hops up and jumps into the pool.*)

Where it was nice and cool. (*Frog 2 swims in the pool for the duration of the poem.*)

Then there were three speckled frogs. (*Each of the three remaining frogs hops up and sits down on the log.*)

Glug, glug! (*The three frogs make a glugging sound.*)

Three little speckled frogs sat on a speckled log. (*The three frogs are sitting on the log.*)

Eating some most delicious bugs. (*The three frogs mime catching and eating bugs.*)

Yum, yum! (*The three frogs rub their tummies.*)

One jumped into the pool, *(Frog 3 hops up and jumps into the pool.)*

Where it was nice and cool, *(Frog 3 swims in the pool for the duration of the poem.)*

Then there were two speckled frogs. *(Each of the two remaining frogs hops up and sits down on the log.)*

Glug, glug! *(The two frogs make a glugging sound.)*

Two little speckled frogs sit on a speckled log. *(The two frogs are sitting on the log.)*

Eating some most delicious bugs. *(The two frogs mime catching and eating bugs.)*

Yum, yum! *(The two frogs rub their tummies.)*

One jumped into the pool, *(Frog 4 hops up and jumps into the pool.)*

Where it was nice and cool, *(Frog 4 swims in the pool for the duration of the poem.)*

Then there was one speckled frog. *(The last frog hops up and sits down on the log.)*

Glug, glug! *(The last frog makes a glugging sound.)*

One little speckled frog sat on a speckled log. *(The last frog is sitting on the log.)*

Eating some most delicious bugs. *(The last frog mimes catching and eating bugs.)*

Yum, yum! *(The five frogs rub their tummies.)*

He jumped into the pool, *(Frog 5 hops up and jumps into the pool.)*

Where it was nice and cool, *(Frog 5 is swims in the pool for the duration of the poem.)*

Then there were no speckled frogs. *(Everyone in the circle shakes their heads.)*

Glug, glug! *(Everyone in the circle makes a glugging sound.)*

My Body Action Song

Directions: This action poem can be sung to the tune of *Twinkle, Twinkle Little Star*. This is a fun way to practice gross motor skills, as well as promote listening skills. When the children get comfortable with the poem they can devise their own actions.

Two little hands go clap, clap, clap (*children clap both hands*).

Two little feet go tap, tap, tap (*children tap both feet*).

One little body turns around (*children turn around*).

One little child sits quietly down (*children to sit down quietly*).

Two little fists thump, thump, thump (*children clench their fists and thump on the floor*).

Two little feet go stomp, stomp, stomp.

One foot goes hop, hop, hop (*children turn around*).

One little child goes squat, squat, squat (*children to squat*).

When I Say

When I say "red," put your hands on your head. (*Children put their hands on their head.*)

When I say "blue," please tie your shoe. (*Children mime tying their shoe.*)

When I say "green," try not to be seen. (*Children hide.*)

When I say "pink," you smell the stink. (*Children hold their noses if they are smelling something really bad*)

When I say "yellow," everyone be mellow. (*Children lie on the floor and relax.*)

When I say "purple," everyone hold hands in a circle. (*Children hold hands in a circle*)

When I say "brown," jump up and then sit down. (*Children jump up and then sit down.*)

If You're Happy and You Know It

Directions: The teacher can add more actions on to this action song. If the children feel comfortable with the actions they can come up with some of their own.

If you're happy and you know it,
Clap your hands. (*Clap, clap*)
If you're happy and you know it,
Clap you're hands. (*Clap, Clap*)
If you're happy and you know it,
Then you're face will surely show it.
If you're happy and you know it
Clap you're hands. (*Clap, Clap*)
If you're happy and you know it,
Stomp you're feet (*Stomp, Stomp*)...
If you're happy and you know it,
Shout "Hooray!" (*Shout "Hooray"*)

Suggestions of different movements:
Jump up high.
Hop down low.
Do the freeze.
Twirl around.
Laugh out loud.
Skip around.
Touch your nose.
Roll on the floor.

Action Poetry/Songs

Five Little Monkeys

Directions: Children get to take turns in acting out this action poem. Six children volunteer. One of the children is the alligator and the other five are the monkeys. The monkeys are numbered from one to five. The rest of the children say the poem.

Five little Monkeys swinging on a tree *(five monkeys are miming swinging on a tree)*,

teasing Mr. Alligator saying, "You can't catch me, no, you can't catch me" *(Five monkeys are making faces at Mr. Alligator).*

Along came Mr. Alligator *(Mr. Alligator tiptoes quietly up to monkey 1)*,

quiet as can be *(spoken very quietly)*,

And *(spoken loudly)*…

(Clap!) *(Mr. Alligator captures monkey 1 and takes him away).*

Four little Monkeys, swinging on a tree *(four monkeys are miming swinging on a tree)*,

teasing Mr. Alligator saying, "You can't catch me, no, you can't catch me" *(four monkeys are making faces at Mr. Alligator).*

Along came Mr. Alligator *(Mr. Alligator tiptoes quietly up to monkey 2)*,

quiet as can be *(spoken very quietly)*,

And *(spoken loudly)*…

(Clap!) *(Mr. Alligator captures monkey 2 and takes him away.)*

Three little Monkeys, swinging on a tree *(three monkeys are miming swinging on a tree)*,

teasing Mr. Alligator saying, "You can't catch me, no, you can't catch me". *(Three monkeys are making faces at the Mr. Alligator.)*

Along came Mr. Alligator *(Mr. Alligator tiptoes quietly up to monkey 3)*

quiet as can be *(spoken very quietly)*,

And *(spoken loudly)*…

(Clap!) *(Mr. Alligator captures monkey 3 and takes him away.)*

Two little Monkeys, swinging on a tree *(two monkeys are miming swinging on a tree)*,

teasing Mr. Alligator saying, "You can't catch me, no, you can't catch me"

(two monkeys are making faces at Mr. Alligator.)

Along came Mr. Alligator *(Mr. Alligator tiptoes quietly up to monkey 4),*

quiet as can be *(spoken very quietly),*

And *(spoken loudly)…*

(Clap!) *(Mr. Alligator captures monkey 4 and takes him away.)*

One little Monkey, swinging on a tree *(one monkey is miming swinging on a tree),*

teasing Mr. Alligator saying, "You can't catch me, no, you can't catch me" *(one monkey is making faces at the alligator.)*

Along came Mr. Alligator *(Mr. Alligator tiptoes quietly up to monkey 5),*

quiet as can be *(spoken very quietly),*

And *(spoken loudly)…*

(Clap!) *(Mr. Alligator captures monkey 5 and takes him away.)*

Everyone: No more monkeys swinging on the tree.

There Was a Princess Long Ago

There was a princess long ago, long, long ago. There was a princess long ago, long, long ago. (*In a circle everyone curtsy/bow and the princess is in the middle dancing.*)

She lived in a big high tower, high tower, high tower. She lived in a big high tower long ago, long, long ago. (*Put hands in "triangle" shape to make tower: princess still dances.*)

A wicked fairy cast a spell, cast a spell, cast a spell. A wicked fairy cast a spell long ago, long, long ago. (*Fairy chases princess about then taps her head casting a spell. (Everyone in the circle casts a spell with their "wands."*)

The princess slept for a hundred years, a hundred years, a hundred years. The princess slept for a hundred years long ago, long, long ago. (*Princess lies in middle of circle sleeping, and everyone puts their head on hands as sleeping action*).

A great big forest grew around, grew around, grew around. A great big forest grew around long ago, long, long ago. (*Children in the circle cross their arms and hold them up in the air.*)

A handsome prince came riding by, riding by, riding by. A handsome prince came riding by long ago, long, long ago. (*Prince runs/gallops round circle and everyone gallops in their spot.*)

He took his sword and cut the trees, cut the trees, cut the trees. He took his sword and cut the trees long ago, long, long ago. (*Prince chops the trees down.*)

He woke the princess with a kiss, with a kiss, with a kiss. He woke the princess with a kiss long ago, long, long ago. (*Prince gives the princess a kiss on head/cheek/lips and everyone blows kisses.*)

The wedding bells go ding dang ding, ding dang ding, ding dang ding. The wedding bells go ding dang, ding long ago, long, long ago. (*All the children pretend to ring bells with their hands; prince and princess dance in middle.*)

And everybody is happy now, happy now, and happy now. And everybody is happy now long ago, long, long ago. (*Everyone is happy, clapping, dancing, jumping, etc.*).

Part Two: Movement Stories

Movement stories are an enjoyable way for children to explore different ways of moving. The stories allow the children to physically express themselves with freedom and imagination. In addition, the movement stories in this book promote key skills, such as listening, teamwork, coordination, balance, strength, flexibility and memory. The following movement stories can be used with children as young as three years old. Each story in this section is clearly laid out. There is an introduction and closure activity for each story and the resources needed are listed at the beginning.

Movement Story One

The Tortoise and the Hare

Resources needed: Clear space and a copy of the story below.
Introduction: Ask the children do they know the story of the tortoise and the hare. Tell them you are going to tell them the story but instead of just sitting and listening they are going to participate in the story. Tell them that they are going to listen for the following words and they have to do the action associated with that word when they hear it in the story. The teacher should explain any words that the children might not understand, such as "boastful"—which is telling everyone how good you are at something. The teacher should go through the different words and their movement. If there are too many words for the age group the teacher can omit some of them. Once the teacher has gone through the words and the actions, she then shouts out words randomly to see if everyone knows the action. The children find their own space in the room so they can move freely and then the story can begin.

Boast/boastful/boasting—stand up straight and puff out chest.
Woods—children make themselves into trees.
Animals—each child chooses a different animal found in the woods and moves like that animal.
Hare—make bunny ears with your hands.
Fast—children move as fast as they can.
Run—run on the spot.
Tortoise—children bend over as if they have something heavy on their back.
Slow—children move in slow motion around the room.

Narrator: Once upon a time there was a very **boastful hare** that lived in the **woods** with lots of other **animals**. He was always **boasting** about how **fast** he could **run**. He **boasted**, "I'm the **fastest** animal in the woods. No one can **run** as **fast** as me." The other **animals** were tired of listening to him. One day the **tortoise** said to the **hare**, "**Hare** you are so **boastful**. I challenge you to a race." **Hare** laughed and said, "**Tortoise**, you will never beat me. You are too **slow** and steady." They decided whoever got to the other side of the **woods** the **fastest** was the winner. All the other **animals** in the **woods** came to watch the race. The **hare ran** as **fast** as he could through the **woods**. After a while he thought to himself, "I'm so **fast** that **slow** tortoise will never beat me. I think I will take a quick nap." Soon he fell asleep. The **tortoise** walked **slowly** through the **woods**.

He passed the sleeping **hare**. The **animals** watched the **tortoise** near the finishing line. The **animals** cheered loudly. The **hare** woke up and **ran** as **fast** as he could through the **woods** to the finishing line but it was too late. The **slow tortoise** had won the race. All the **animals** in the **woods** congratulated the **tortoise**. The **hare** had to remind himself that he shouldn't **boast** about his **fast** pace because **slow** and steady won the race.

Closure: Do you think the hare was boastful after the race? Why not? What lesson did we learn from the story? Now I want you to be your chosen animal again. All the animals stand in a straight line. The teacher explains that they are going to have a race but they must move in slow motion.

Movement Story Two

The Three Little Pigs

Resources needed: Clear space and a copy of the story below.
Introduction: Ask the children if they know the story of the little pigs. Tell them you are going to tell them the story but instead of just sitting and listening they are going to participate in the story. Tell them that they are going to listen for the following words and they have to do the action associated with that word when they hear it in the story. The teacher should go through the different words and their movement. If there are too many words for the age group the teacher can omit some of them. The teacher goes through the words and the actions then tests randomly to see if everyone knows the action. When the children are ready they must find their own space in the room so they can move freely.

Any number—show that number of fingers.
Little—crouch down as small as you can.
Pig—get on all fours and oink once.
Pigs—get on all fours and oink twice.
Big—stretch up as high as you can.
Bad—make an angry face.
Wolf—make hands into claws and say "aargh."
Laughing—laugh loudly.
Smiling—big wide smile.
Trotted—trot up and down the space.
Straw—rub your hands together.
Sticks—clap your hands together.
Bricks—clap your hands on your thighs.
Huff/huffed— – blow.
Puff/puffed—blow harder.
Blow\blew—stamp feet on the ground.

Narrator: Once upon a time there was a mother **pig** that lived with her **three little pigs**. One day she said "**Little pigs,** I think it is time for you to leave and make your own way in this **big** world. You each need to build your own **house**." The little pigs were very excited about their new, **big** adventure. Mother **pig** gave each of her **little pigs** a hug but she warned them "Remember to watch out for the **big bad wolf**." The **little pigs** waved goodbye to their mother and they **trotted** into the woods. They were **laughing** and **smiling** and soon they came across a man who was carrying some **straw**. The **first little pig** said "may I have some **straw** to build my **house**." The man said kindly, "Of course, you may." The man gave the **first little pig** some **straw** to build his house. Just before they left the man warned them, "Watch out for the **big bad wolf**." The **first little pig** built his **house** of straw. The **two** other **pigs trotted** on down the road. They were **laughing** and **smiling** and soon they came across a man who was carrying some **sticks**. The **second little pig** said, "May I have some **sticks** to build my **house**." The man said kindly, "Of course, you may." The man gave the **second** little **pig** some **sticks** to build his house. Just before they left the man warned them, "Watch out for the **big bad wolf**." The **second little pig** built his **house** of sticks. The **third little pig trotted** on down the road. He was laughing and **smiling** and soon he came across a man who was carrying some **bricks**. The third little pig said, "May I have some **bricks** to build my house." The man said kindly, "Of course, you may." The man gave the **third little pig** some **bricks** to build his **house**. Just before they left the man warned him, "Watch out for the **big bad wolf**."

The **third** little **pig** built his **house** of **bricks**. The **first little pig** had just finished building his **house** of straw when the **big bad wolf** appeared. He said, **"Little pig, little pig**, let me come in." The **first little pig** replied, "Not by the hair of my chinny, chin, chin." Then the **wolf** said, "I'll **huff** and I'll **puff** and I will **blow** the **house** down." So he **huffed** and he **puffed** and he **blew** the **house** down. The **first little pig trotted** very quickly to his brother's **house** made of **sticks**. The **second** little **pig** had just finished building his **house** of **sticks** when he heard a knock on the door and to his surprise it was his brother. All of a sudden the **big bad wolf** appeared. He said **"Little pig, little pig**, let me come in." The **second little pig** replied, "Not by hair of my chinny, chin, chin." Then the **wolf** said, "I'll **huff** and I'll **puff** and I will **blow** the house down." So he **huffed** and he **puffed** and he **blew** the **house** down. The **two** little **pigs trotted** very quickly to their brother's house made of **bricks**.

The **third little pig** had just finished building his **house** of **bricks** when he heard a knock on the door and to his surprise it was his **two** brothers. All of a sudden, the **big bad wolf** appeared. He said, "**Little pig, little pig**, let me come in." The **third** little **pig** replied, "Not by hair of my chinny, chin, chin." Then the **wolf** said, "Then I'll **huff** and I'll **puff** and I will **blow** the **house** down." The wolf **huffed** and he **puffed**. He **huffed** and he **puffed** but he couldn't **blow** the **house** down. He heard the **three little pigs** inside the **house.** They were **laughing**. This made the **wolf** very angry indeed. He decided he would climb to the top of the roof and come down the chimney. The **third little pig** heard him on the roof and he came up with a clever plan. He put a **big** pot of boiling water on the fire which was just underneath the chimney. The **wolf** came tumbling down the chimney and landed into the **big** pot of boiling water and "SPLASH!" That was the end of the **big bad wolf**. The **three little pigs** lived happily ever after.

Closure: Ask the children what they think happened to the big bad wolf? Where did he go when he ran out of the house? Do you think he ever tried to blow down houses again? Do you think he learned his lesson?

Movement Story Three

The Magical Music Shop

Resources needed: Clear space, triangle and pictures of different types of instruments (optional).

Introduction: Tell the children they are going to participate in a movement story about a magical music shop. Show them pictures of different type of instruments. Discuss different kind of musical instrument families.

Brass instruments are made of brass or another metal and they make sound when air is blown into them. The instruments in the brass family include trumpet, trombone, tuba, French horn, cornet, and bugle.

Percussion instruments usually make sound when they are hit or shaken. The instruments in the percussion family include drums, cymbals, triangle, tambourine, chimes, bells, and xylophone.

String instruments are made with strings. The strings may be struck, plucked or bowed. The instruments in this family include violin, viola, cello, bass, and harp.

Woodwind instruments make sound when air is blown inside or across them and vibrates. Woodwind instruments include flute, clarinet, recorder, bassoon, and oboe.

Ask the children what their favourite instrument is? If they could be an instrument what would it be? Why did they choose it? What sound does their chosen instrument make? If their instrument could move how would it move? What kind of musical family does their chosen instrument belong to? Make sure everyone has a chance to explain their choice. Before the story starts get one of the children to volunteer to be the music shop owner. The teacher is the narrator. The rest of the children are their chosen instruments.

Narrator: Once upon a time there was a very special music shop. The music shop was special because all the instruments that lived in the shop were magic. *(The children all freeze in the shape of their instrument.)* The music shop owner loved his instruments very much. He treated them with tender loving care. *(The owner goes around the shop. He polishes and dusts all the instruments.)* Every night the owner would close the shop and go upstairs to bed. *(The shop owner goes off to bed and lies on the floor and falls asleep. He snores loudly.)* What the owner didn't know was when the clock struck midnight the instruments would come alive. *(Narrator tinkles the* *triangle.)* The magic instruments would come down from their shelves and out from the window display. *(The instruments start to move slowly out of their positions.)* They would all play together. *(The instruments start playing their music and moving around interacting with one another.)* The instruments were so happy when they were with their friends. They had so much fun and nobody knew about their magic powers. Every morning when the instruments heard the music shop owner's footsteps *(the owner makes loud stomping noises with his feet)* they would quickly run back to their places on the shelves or in the window display. *(The instruments go back to their original positions and freeze.)* Every morning the music shop owner would walk around the shop inspecting his instruments and every morning he would rub his head and say, "That's funny. I thought I had put the violin on that shelf, or didn't I leave the drum on the window." But the music shop owner never suspected a thing and every night when he went to bed and the clock struck midnight the instruments would play to their hearts content. *(The instruments come out and play.)* Every morning the music shop owner would come and they would quickly move back to their places. *(The instruments move quickly back to their positions.) (The narrator can say this section as many times as he wants.)*

After a while the music shop owner knew something was not quite right. So one morning he tiptoed into the shop and he found the instruments all playing together. *(The owner tiptoes very quietly into the shop.)* He heard the most beautiful sound he had ever heard. He said, "Oh my, what a wonder. I have a good idea. Everyone line up. We are going to make a marching band and we will show the whole town what magic instruments are in this shop." All the instruments lined up and they marched through the town making their magic music. *(The instruments line up behind each other and march around the space playing their music.)*

Closure: The teacher takes on the role of a local journalist. He has heard about the magic music shop and wants to interview the instruments and the shop owner. At the end everyone makes a still image for the photograph in the newspaper. Get the children to think of an appropriate headline.

Movement Story Four

Rhino Chase

Resource needed: Clear space, pictures of rhinos (optional.)

Facts about Rhinos:
A rhinoceroses is the second largest land mammal on Earth. The elephant is the largest. There are five species of rhinos, two African and three Asian. The African species are the white and black rhino. The Asian species are the Indian, Javan, and Sumatran rhino. The African rhinos have two horns and the Asian rhinos generally have one horn, except for the Sumatran rhino which has two horns. Rhinos range from 1.8 metres (6 feet) to 3.6 metres (12 feet) in length and 1.2metres (4 feet) to 1.9 metres (6.5 feet) tall. Their weight ranges from 59kgs (1300lbs) to 770kgs (1700lbs). Their life expectancy is 35 years. Rhinos can run up to 48 kilometres (30 miles) per hour. Rhinos only eat plants. There are only about 30,000 rhinos left in the world. They are an endangered species. They are often hunted for their horns, which are seen as very valuable. The most important thing to remember is if you are chased by a rhino you must run in a zig-zag pattern as rhinos can only see straight in front of them.

Introduction: Ask the children what they know about rhinos. Show them pictures of rhinos and share some of the facts above with the children. Tell the children we are going on a rhino chase. Remind them what they must do if a rhino chases them. They must run in a zig-zag direction. Everyone practices running in a zig-zag direction. Teach them the following rhyme which they will chant as they go on their rhino chase.

Chant: We are going on a rhino chase, rhino chase, rhino chase.
We are so fast.
So very, very fast! Once they know the chant the chase can begin.

Narrator: Today, children we are going on a rhino chase. What do we need to bring with us in our backpacks? Have you any suggestions? Sunglasses, sun cream, binoculars, sandwiches, water, etc. *(Children mime putting their objects into their backpacks and then they stand in a straight line.)*

Narrator: Are we ready? Now let everyone sing. *(Everybody move around in a circle singing the chant.)*

Chant: We are going on a rhino chase, rhino chase, rhino chase.
We are so fast.
So very, very fast!

Narrator: It is rainy season in the jungle so there is mud everywhere. *(Narrator stops suddenly.)* Look, what do we see? We see brown sticky mud? We must try to go through it. It is very sticky and gooey. We are stuck. Help, we are sinking. *(The children go through the mud but they get stuck and start to sink. They start to pull each other out. They hold on to their friends and finally get each other out but they still haven't been able to get through it.)* Finally, everyone is out of the mud, but we can't get through it by ourselves. We need help. I know. Let's climb up on these elephants *(points to imaginary elephants)* because elephants are strong and tall and can get through the mud. Everybody climb up on your elephant. *(Everybody climbs onto their elephant and rides through the mud. The elephants move slowly through the mud.)* Everybody climb off your elephant slowly. Shake off the mud. Is everyone ready? Off we go. *(Everyone chants.)*

Chant: We are going on a rhino chase, rhino chase, rhino chase.
We are so fast.
So very, very fast!

Narrator: Oh dear, look it is a long deep river. We have to swim through it. Everyone let's get ready and dive in and swim across. *(Everybody jumps in and starts swimming.)* The water is very rough, today. Everyone is getting bashed from left to right. *(Children move from left to right and are struggling to swim.)* We have to return to the river bank. *(The children pull each other out of the river. Everybody is lying on the river bank trying to catch their breath.)* How will get over to the other side? I see crocodiles. We can jump on them and we will arrive safely across the water. *(The children hop on the crocodiles and they get across to other side and they alight safely.)* We are all wet and we need to dry off before we continue our journey. *(The children start to shake their bodies until they are dry.)* Is everybody ready? If so let's go. *(Everybody chants.)*

Chant: We are going on a rhino chase, rhino chase, rhino chase.
We are so fast.
So very, very fast!

Narrator: Now, look it is a deep dark jungle with big thick trees. We must try to go through them. Everybody take out your knives and we will cut down the trees. *(The children mime taking out their knives and then try to cut down the trees.)* It is very difficult. Everybody is getting tired and thirsty. We must make sure we drink our water because the sun is very hot today. *(Everybody drinks their water.)* This is too difficult. The trees in this jungle are too thick. I think we have to turn back. Listen, what do we hear? *(Everybody puts their hands on their ears.)* We hear some monkeys and look *(points upwards);* they are swinging from the trees above. I have an idea. We can swing from branch to branch just like the

Rhino Chase

monkeys and we will get through this jungle. *(Everyone swings from tree to tree.)* Everybody make the sound of the monkeys. At last, we are out of the big thick jungle. *(The children climb down from the trees.)* Everybody let's continue on our way. *(Everybody chants.)*

Chant: We are going on a rhino chase, rhino chase, rhino chase.
We are so fast.
So very, very fast!

Narrator: It is getting even hotter and now we are hungry *(everybody rubs their tummies.)* It is lunch time. *(The children take out their lunch and starts eating it. The narrator asks the children individually what they had for lunch.)* Is everybody full? We should have a quick nap before we continue. *(Everybody stretches and yawns and lies on the ground. Everyone is asleep and snoring.)* I feel something next to us. Everybody keep your eyes closed and put your hands out to feel whatever is next to us. *(The children start feeling around the floor with their eyes shut.)* What do we feel? We feel four hard feet, some very thick leathery skin and then a very pointed and sharp horn. Everybody open your eyes. It is a great big fierce rhino. Everybody run zigzag through the jungle. The rhino is coming after us. There is the thick jungle. Everybody climb a tree. The rhino is banging on the tree so we have to hold on tight. Everybody swing zigzag from tree to tree like the monkeys and we can get out of the thick jungle. Is everybody out of jungle? The rhino is still following us. Everybody run to the river. Jump on the crocodiles. Crocodiles, swim zig-zag across the river. The rhino has jumped into the river and is still following us. He seems very angry. We are out of the river but we must keep running because the rhino is following closely behind. Climb on the elephants. Elephants go zig-zag across the mud. Quick, everyone climb down from the elephants and run as fast as you can to our jungle lodge. Remember to run in a zig-zag fashion. We are here at last. Shut the door, lock the windows and hid under the bed. Now we are safe we can relax and fall asleep.

Closure: Everybody imagines that they are a rhino, and that they are being chased by hunters. How would they move? How would they sound? If they could talk, what would they say to the hunters? They make a still image of a rhino being chased by hunters. The teacher taps them on the shoulder and they must say how they feel about being chased.

Movement Story Five

The Seed That Didn't Want to Grow

Resources needed: Clear space, different types of flowers (if you have access to them) or pictures of different types of flowers, seeds, lively music

Introduction: Show the children the seeds. Pass the seeds around the class. Let them touch and feel them. Ask the children what they think the seed will go grow into? Show them the flowers. Ask them what do they think the seed needed to grow into a flower? Give each child a chance to speak. Ask the children questions such as, if they were a flower, what type of flower would they be and why? Tell the children they are going to be a tiny little seed. The teacher gets everybody to find their own space. The children stretch their arms out and make sure they are not touching anyone. When everybody has found their space they must make themselves as small as possible, so the story can begin. The teacher is the narrator and must allow for long pauses so that children can express themselves through physical movement.

Narrator: You are a tiny seed that is buried deep below the ground. *(The children all curl up as small and as tight as they can in their own space.)* It is winter time and it is very, very cold. *(The children all shiver.)* There is lots of wind and rain. *(The children get up and move around the room, moving their bodies in circles and going faster and faster as they clap their hands on their legs to make the rain sound.)* When the seed hears all this noise he curls up tighter and tighter. *(The children find their space again and curl up as tight as they can.)* After a while, spring arrives and the weather begins to get warmer. The seed feels the warmth of spring. *(The children start to stretch out very slowly.)* There are some light rain showers. *(The children tap their feet lightly on the ground.)* Summer comes and the seed gets bigger and bigger and finally it bursts through the earth. *(The children are in a crouched position and then they move up slowly. They must give a big push before they eventually get through the earth.)* The seed feels the rays of the sun and it slowly turn into a beautiful flower. *(The children stand up fully and turn into a flower.)* The flower gets very hot. *(The children wipe their brows.)* The flower gets sprayed with water. *(The children feel the water being sprayed on them.)* The flower gets bigger and stronger. *(The children make themselves as tall as possible.)* The flower loves the light and sun. Whenever there was a light summer wind he danced beautifully. *(The children dance around the room.)* Soon, autumn comes and the petals fall off the flower and it gets smaller and smaller until eventually the flower is no more, but there is a little seed that goes underground and curls up,

The Seed That Didn't Want to Grow

waiting for winter to come. *(The children get smaller and smaller until they are back in their space, curled up tightly.)*

Closure: The teacher plays some music. The children imagine that they are flowers dancing, and they must free dance to the music.

Movement Story Six

Adventure in Space

Resources needed: Clear space, balloons, flags, and objects for the moon (optional).

Introduction: Tell the children that they are going to become astronauts. Explain what an astronaut is or show them pictures of an astronaut in space. An astronaut is a person who is trained to travel in space. Discuss some interesting facts about astronauts with the children.

Ten interesting facts about astronauts:
- Yuri Gagarin was the first man to travel in space in 1961. He was Russian. His space shuttle was called "Vostok 1."
- John Glenn was the first American to travel in space in 1962. His space shuttle was called "Friendship 7."
- Laika, a stray dog trained by the Russians, was the first living thing to go into space. Unfortunately he died a few hours after launch. Ham, the chimp, was the first animal taken into space by an American astronaut. He arrived safely back to earth after 16 hours in space.
- In space you float because there is no gravity. The inner ear doesn't need to keep you balanced. When astronauts come back from space they are very clumsy.
- In space, there is no gravity to weigh you down so your spine stretches and relaxes, and the astronaut can grow up to 5cm. or 2 inches.
- In space the sun rises every 90 minutes.
- Astronauts in space can see other planets without a telescope.
- In space it is not possible to breathe air normally. The space suits have oxygen attached to them to help astronauts breathe when they are outside the space shuttle.
- The longest time an astronaut has spent in space is 2 years and 73 days.
- Astronauts have to sleep in buckled bunk beds. If they are not strapped to the bed they will float when they are asleep, as there isn't any gravity.

The teacher discusses with the children that they are going to go on a special mission to space. Ask for suggestions for the name of their space shuttle. Ask them how they will move in space as there is no gravity. They must move in slow motion with their space suits. Get the children to practice moving around the room very slowly. Get them to jump up and down in slow motion. Once they are used to the slow movements, the story can begin. The teacher will be the pilot.

Pilot: Astronauts, this is space shuttle *(name of the space shuttle)*. My name is *(pilot's name)*. I am your pilot for this important top-secret space mission. *(All the astronauts walk on to the shuttle and take their positions on the floor.)* Welcome on board the *(name of the space shuttle)*. Our flight time will be *(time)* and we will be flying at an altitude of *(altitude)*, at a speed of *(speed)*. At this time all electronic devices must be switched off or set to space shuttle mode. *(All the astronauts take out their devices and mime switching them off.)* Please take your seat and fasten your seat belt. *(The astronauts lie on the floor with their feet in the air.)* Astronauts, please prepare for blast off. Everybody count down 10, 9, 8, 7, 6, 5, 4, 3, 2, 1, BLAST OFF. *(Everybody count from 10 to 1 and creates a loud explosive sound.)* Keep your seat belts on as there is a lot of turbulence. *(Astronauts are shaking from side to side while fastening their seats.)* We have reached a height of (height). The seat belt sign has been switched off. *(The astronauts take off their seat belts, and because there is no gravity they start moving in slow motion and imagine that they are floating. They go forwards and backwards, up and down, side to side as they look out of the windows.)* Astronauts, due to a technical problem with the space shuttle we have to make an emergency landing on the moon. Everyone, please take your seats as quickly as possible. *(The astronauts sit back in their seats and put their seat belts on.)* Everyone hold on tight. *(They make an emergency stop and they all go forward and backward.)* We are going to be stuck on the moon until we manage to fix the technical problem with the space shuttle. If you would like, you can put on your space suit and go for a walk on the moon. *(The astronauts put on their space suits.)* Remember to use your oxygen masks. *(Everyone puts on their oxygen mask.)* You have to move slowly on the moon because you don't want your space suits to burst open. *(They all get off the rocket carefully.)* Everyone take your time going down the space shuttle steps. Hold on tight. Now that we are on the moon we should put our country's flag on the moon. We should all take something from the moon as a souvenir. *(Astronauts move around the room carefully and slowly and they mime picking up something and putting it in their space suit pocket.)* Oh, look, it is a meteorite. *(Teacher throws a balloon in the air which represents a meteorite.)* Astronauts, we must make sure that the meteorite doesn't hit the moon as it will cause a crater. *(The astronauts try to keep the balloon from hitting the floor. They work together. The teacher can keep adding meteorites or balloons until they start to drop on the floor and cause craters.)* It has turned into a meteorite shower and it is getting worse, and we have to run to the rocket to take cover. *(They run as fast as they can in the space suits. Remember they can burst them* *if they run too fast. They all climb the stairs and get back into the rocket.)* Welcome abroad. Please take your seats and fasten your seatbelts. *(They lie on the backs with the feet up.)* Count down begins 10, 9, 8, 7, 6, 5, 4, 3, 2, 1, lift off. *(They count down and make the sound of the engine taking off. They slowly begin to sit up as the rocket levels off and is floating through space.)* The seatbelt sign has been switched off. Everyone look out the window. Remember what you see so you can tell everybody on Earth. *(The children take off their seatbelts and look out the window.)* Astronauts, it is time to return to Earth. Everyone fasten your seatbelts. I hope you enjoyed this space flight and will join us again in the future. *(They land safely and everyone alights from the space shuttle.)*

Closure: The children sit in a circle. One by one they take out their souvenir from the moon and explain what it is, what it looks like, or what it feels like? Each child says what they saw or experienced in space.

Movement Story Seven

The Clumsy Elephant and the Beautiful Ballet Shoes

Resources needed: Clear space, some classical music (optional).

Introduction: The teacher tells the children that they are going to hear a story about a clumsy elephant. The children should find their own space and they have to listen very carefully.

Narrator: There once was an elephant that was different from all the other elephants in the jungle, as he could only walk on two feet instead of four. So he wasn't very good at balancing since he didn't walk on four feet. *(All the children walk around like the elephant with two legs and they lose their balance and fall down.)* One day, he decided to go for a walk in the jungle. He heard the monkeys in the trees above. *(Children move like monkey and make monkey sounds.)* Then he heard snakes hissing in the grass *(children move like snakes and make hissing noises)*, and finally he heard the lions roaring from their caves *(children move like the lions and roar loudly.)* He kept walking until he came across a pair of beautiful ballet shoes. What colour were they? *(Children answer. The ballet shoes are magic so they can be any colour.)* The elephant never saw such beautiful shoes. He rushed to put the ballet shoes on. *(Children put on the ballet shoes.)* He looked at them and admired them. He started to dance gracefully in them. *(Children move/dance gracefully around the room.)* He was so happy because he was known as the "clumsy elephant." But all of a sudden the shoes had a life of their own. They made him jump up and down, up and down. *(Children jump up and down, up and down, up and down.)* The elephant sat down and the ballet shoes eventually stopped moving. He got up slowly and the shoes were very still, but once he got up on two feet again the shoes went from side to side. *(Children move from left to right, left to right, left to right.)* They went faster and faster from side to side until eventually the clumsy elephant sat down. *(Children sit down.)* He got up slowly and the shoes were slow. *(Children get up slowly and carefully.)* When he was on two feet the shoes went round in circles faster and faster until suddenly they stopped. *(Children go round in circles.)* The elephant tiptoed slowly and then the shoes went up and down, from side to side, and around in circles faster and faster each time until they suddenly stopped. *(Children tiptoe and jump up and down, move from side to side, and around in circles.)* Then the shoes started to dance very gracefully. *(Children dance very gracefully.)* The elephant had never been so graceful. The monkey came down from the trees. The snake came out of the grass, and the lion came out of the cave. They all agreed they had never seen an elephant so graceful. When he had finished his dance he took a bow. *(Children take a bow.)* And bent down and kissed his shoes. He said, "Thank you, beautiful ballet shoes." *(Children kiss their shoes.)*

Closure: Tell the children that the elephant is very tired and he is going to go to sleep with his ballet shoes. *(Everyone lies down on the floor and kisses their ballet shoes good night. They stay very still as if they were asleep.)* The teacher moves around the room trying to get the elephants to move. If an elephant moves then they have to get up and help the teacher to get the other sleeping elephants to move. They are not allowed to touch the other elephants, but they may move close and try to get them to laugh by talking to them.

Printed in Great Britain
by Amazon